WHAT IS A SCHIZOPHRENIC SUPPOSED TO LOOK LIKE?

Third Edition

Lori Rochat

Copyright © 2017 by Lori Rochat

What Is A Schizophrenic Supposed To Look Like?

Third Edition

Lori Rochat, Author

Jill M. Riga, Contributing Editor

Michael T. Petro, Jr., General Editor

PetroPublications.com

Front & Back Cover Photo
© Photoeuphoria | Dreamstime Stock Photos

Published in the United States of America

ISBN-10: 1548307122

ISBN-13: 978-1548307127

All rights reserved solely by the author. No part of this book may be reproduced, stored in a retrieval system, or transmitted in any form or by any means, including electronic, mechanical, photocopy, recording, scanning, or any other, without prior written permission from the author, except for reviewers and researchers who may quote brief passages.

Dedication

I dedicate this book to my mother for helping me with the topic selections for this book. In addition, I am eternally grateful to her for being there for me throughout life's struggles, and for guiding me on my path toward wellness. My Aunt Carol must also receive recognition for referring me to Dr. Herbert Meltzer's study, which dramatically improved my life. Also, I would like to thank Matt Sucre from the Cleveland Public Library for helping me to get started with this project and for referring me to Jill M. Riga, a contributing editor to this book. Lastly, I wish to thank Michael T. Petro, Jr., an author, editor, and publisher at Petro Publications. He served as the general editor and helped me make this book become a reality.

Table Of Contents

Introduction..1

What Is A Schizophrenic Supposed To Look Like?.....................2

What Is A High-Functioning Schizophrenic?..............................3

Schizophrenia: Let's Call It Something Else!..............................4

My Life Before Schizophrenia..5

Schizophrenia: Are You One In One Hundred?.........................6

My Medical Records...9

Getting Your Medical Records..11

What It's Like To Have Schizophrenia......................................12

Understanding Voices..13

Panic Disorder..14

Schizophrenia And Street Drugs..15

Schizophrenia And Smoking..15

Suicide And Schizophrenia...16

Violence And Schizophrenia..17

Schizophrenia And The Police..18

Doctors...19

Forensic Psychiatry..20

Medication..20

Schizophrenia And Drug Interactions...23

Nutrition And Health..24

Supplements 28

Recipes..29

Fitness And Medication..32

Grooming And Schizophrenia...32

Dating And Schizophrenia..33

People May Use Your Illness Against You..33

Stigma And Discrimination...33

Schizophrenia And The Workplace...36

Volunteering On The Mental Ward..36

Where To Go For Psychiatric Help In The Cleveland,

Ohio Area..37

Additional Support Services...39

Movies About Schizophrenia You Should Consider Watching........41

Reading Material About Schizophrenia You Should

Consider Reviewing...44

Group Homes And Housing...44

My Mom's Advice To Other Mothers 45

Denial 46

How To Avoid Relapse 46

Schizophrenia And God 47

So, What Is A Schizophrenic Supposed To Look Like? 48

Special Notes From The Author 50

About The Author 52

Introduction

I would like the reader to understand my motivation for writing this book. The diagnosis of schizophrenia can be as disturbing as the symptoms one experiences with this form of illness. I wrote this book because every life experience I have had relates to my mental illness in some way, and I wish to share those experiences with others. I love helping people and have compassion for the mentally ill. I understand the challenges they face and have a deep desire to help them deal with those challenges as effectively as possible.

I am also very passionate about changing the name of schizophrenia for at least two reasons. Firstly, most people cannot spell this strange sounding word. Secondly, the word schizophrenia is scary to many people and it conjures up stereotypic images of a gloomy or dangerous individual. I titled my book, *What is a Schizophrenic Supposed to Look Like?* to shine a little light on the fact that the general public often comes into contact with schizophrenics in their daily lives — but they are unable to distinguish them from non-schizophrenics! They are unable to spot them in a crowd!

So, to help end the widespread misunderstanding people have about schizophrenia and to stop the stigmatization that follows, I would like readers to ask themselves, "What is a schizophrenic supposed to look like?" I want them to know that when they describe a schizophrenic in stereotypic terms, they are usually wrong because it is not a "look!"

What Is A Schizophrenic Supposed To Look Like?

There is a website, *www.schizophrenia.com*, where people with schizophrenia can communicate with others who have the same illness. Sometimes people say to me when I am stabilized on my meds, "You don't look schizophrenic." So my question to the people on this website was, "What is a schizophrenic supposed to look like?" I received some interesting responses.

Most all who responded admitted that they didn't know what a schizophrenic is supposed to look like although they had schizophrenia themselves. One respondent said that an individual with schizophrenia was someone who dressed in old clothing and didn't wash too often. Another stated that he looked normal but he dressed in black "like a Sith," which as Star Wars fans know is an alien race with a terrifying appearance and devoted to "the Dark Side." One reported that he "looks okay" except for some involuntary jaw movements and as one would expect, he found these movements to be "annoying." Lastly, an individual said that he can "blend in well" with others on the job or at a restaurant. He also stated that he "fits in so well" most anywhere that he wonders if "maybe the guy sitting next to me in the restaurant is a schizophrenic blending in too!"

At this point, I would like to state that people with physical disabilities, such as those in wheelchairs, cannot hide their disabilities. But because mental illness is an internal disability, it can be hidden from the public. Yet people with schizophrenia who are not stabilized on medication do expose their mental disability when they talk to themselves or talk to someone who is not there.

It appears that when people with schizophrenia are asked, "What is a schizophrenic supposed to look like?" the answer is unclear, based on responses provided at *www.schizophrenia.com*.

What Is A High-Functioning Schizophrenic?

The second question I asked people who subscribed to the website *www.schizophrenia.com* was as follows: "What is a high-functioning schizophrenic?" Once again, I received some very interesting responses.

One respondent said, "I consider myself a high-functioning schizophrenic. I own a home, own a car, have been married, and have raised a child. I rely on medicine to get through the day, but I am not in intensive therapy. I make my own decisions and can feed, dress, and entertain myself."

After trying three different medications one female respondent said, "I'm high-functioning." She added, "Life is normal. I have friends, work, have a degree and I'm thinking of going to grad school." She says the guys she dates sometimes "crack crazy people jokes" and they "have no clue" she has schizophrenia. When not taking her medication she suffers from delusions and she hears voices. When taking medications that didn't work, she said that "life really sucked!" However, now that she has found a medication that works, "Life is just fine," as long as she takes her medication.

Some stated that they may be high-functioning sometimes but not at all times because they have good days and bad days.

Schizophrenia: Let's Call It Something Else!

My mom and I agree that we do not like the term schizophrenia. Over the years, people have come to identify schizophrenia as a totally scary word. When people hear the words schizophrenia or schizophrenic, they automatically think these words mean the same thing as "crazy," "lunatic," "insane," or "psychopath." Did you know that schizophrenia used to be called "dementia praecox?" My mom had an old dictionary, *The Reader's Digest Great Encyclopedic Dictionary*, published by Funk and Wagnall in 1975. Here is its definition for schizophrenia: "Any group of psychotic disorders characterized by delusional formations, a retreat from reality, conflicting emotions, and deterioration of personality; formerly called dementia praecox." We feel neither label is accurate. We think it should be called "thought disorder," because that is precisely what is experienced by the individual. One's thoughts are confused and disordered. People with schizophrenia have difficulty distinguishing between what is real and what is imaginary, and that can be very confusing!

Bill MacPhee, the publisher of *SZ Magazine* (formerly known as *Schizophrenia Digest*), launched a campaign in 2015 to change the name of schizophrenia in order to stop the stigma. He mentions in an online article that the image the public has of a person with schizophrenia is that of a potentially violent killer or a disheveled homeless person wandering the streets. Many have suggested the label should be changed to "salience syndrome." Salience syndrome refers to the process wherein both internal and external stimuli are consciously experienced. He has suggested the mental health community adopt the term "MacPhee syndrome," supposedly to "put a face" on this form of illness.

Because Bill MacPhee has been diagnosed with schizophrenia, but is a successful, high-functioning person who publishes *SZ Magazine*, he believes "MacPhee syndrome" would convey the message that people with this illness are not scary, dysfunctional people.

Many people believe schizophrenia means split personality, and I agree that the term "split personality" may apply to schizophrenia because when not on medication people with this illness can talk normal one minute and not normal the next minute. So it appears as if more than one personality is operating within a single individual. It should also be noted that you cannot talk people with schizophrenia out of their intrusive thoughts; the only thing that can control intrusive thoughts is medication.

I hope this book will inspire mental health professionals to replace the term schizophrenia with a label that is descriptive but not frightening and not misunderstood by the general public. I think it would be a relief to all who have received the diagnosis of schizophrenia! Again, we feel "thought disorder" is the most appropriate name for this illness.

My Life Before Schizophrenia

My childhood was basically normal except for perhaps a few unusual circumstances. Unfortunately, my father died when I was only eight years old. My mother, a secretary at that time, faced the task of raising me and my brother by herself. Her company moved a lot, and as a consequence, so did we!

During high school summer break I got a job at Mr. Chicken at the age of 16. I loved that job! After graduating from high school I stayed at my grandmother's house and got a job at a hotel. During this time period I had no idea what I wanted to do with my life even though I studied cosmetology in high school. While staying with my grandmother she began to notice unusual behavior on my part. For example, I would stay awake all night listening to music. My grandmother called my mom to come get me and take me home because of my bizarre behavior. This signified the beginning of my struggle with mental illness.

Schizophrenia: Are You One In One Hundred?

Did you know that one in one hundred people have schizophrenia? Schizophrenia is a thought disorder characterized by delusions, hallucinations, paranoia, and social isolation. Schizophrenia can be controlled with medication, but there is no known cure at this time. There are many drugs available for the treatment of schizophrenia, but drug treatment must be tailored for each individual. Each patient has a unique body chemistry that reacts differently to various medications. Symptoms of schizophrenia tend to appear between the ages of 16 and sometimes well into the late 30's. There are several different types of schizophrenia, but I personally suffer from paranoid schizophrenia so that is the only type I will discuss.

Now I am going to tell you the story of how I found out I had schizophrenia. No one in my family and none of my friends ever had or understood schizophrenia. It started when I was 17 years old. I was getting panic attacks, and my grades in high school started to deteriorate. I became depressed and suicidal. After high school, I started experiencing paranoia and delusional thoughts. For example, I thought my neighbors were spying on me, my phone was bugged, and that there were cameras in the house. I thought my mother was putting poison in my food, people could read my mind, and I thought the TV and newspapers were about me.

In addition, I was laughing at things that were not funny. I was hearing voices telling me I was psychic, and I was not sleeping well. My mother thought I was on street drugs, so she said she wanted to take me to the hospital for drug testing. I told her I was not taking any street drugs, but she did not believe me so she took me to the hospital anyway. They drug-tested me and discovered I had no drugs in my system. I was mad at my mom for taking me there and I did not want to stay. At that time, I could not recognize that I had a problem because with schizophrenia, you often can't understand that you are the one with the problem. I kicked my mom's chair and told her she was crazy for taking me there.

This is how I learned about involuntary admission, or the placement of a person under psychiatric care without their consent. If mentally ill people or people addicted to alcohol or other drugs are out of control, aggressive, or at serious risk of harming themselves or others, they can be involuntarily admitted to receive treatment. This is the point at which you would call the police and ask for a CIT-trained police officer, as discussed in the section "Schizophrenia and the Police."

Once admitted, I tried to get off the mental ward when someone opened the door. I simply snuck out. I started to run and make a phone call to a friend, telling her to come get me, but two police officers found me and brought me back to the mental ward. The hospital staff told my mom to leave and they locked me up in a room with only a bed. My first thought was, "How can I escape?" There was a window that I thought I could jump out of, but there was no way to open it and it was far too high to reach. When the hospital staff opened my door, I tried to push them away and escape, but I did not succeed.

Eventually the hospital staff opened my door and said, "If you remain calm, we will let you out of your room." I said, "Okay," because I felt like I was in jail. I wandered around and asked a guy on the mental ward, "What are you in here for?" He said, "Schizophrenia!" I was so afraid of him that I would not go near him. Later, I was told that I had schizophrenia, and all I remember is the hospital staff telling me I needed to take a medication called Haldol.

Finally, after three long months, they released me. One year after being discharged from this Cleveland-area hospital, I joined Dr. Herbert Meltzer's study to test a new drug called clozapine (Clozaril). This was an outpatient program that lasted two years. While in this outpatient program, I learned that research trials are a great way to test a variety of new drugs to see which ones work best for you.

When the two-year study was over, they took me off clozapine to try other medications. I wound up in the hospital again for another three months. This time it was not as scary because I had become an experienced hospital inpatient. Again, I felt like I was in prison. I remember I wanted to get out of there so badly I started screaming, "Let me out of here!" They moved me to a room with just a mattress and padded walls. I remember crying and crying. When I calmed down, they let me back onto the general ward.

A mental hospital can be scary at times because some of the other patients can be very intimidating. For example, one female patient wanted to pick a fight with me, and a male patient tried to rape me. The hospital staff moved him to another floor. After three long months, they put me back on clozapine and I was released once again. Without my medication, my life would be horrible. I always say to myself, "Schizophrenia is the curse, and the medicine is the blessing."

My Medical Records

My medical records from my hospitalization in 1990 fill a huge notebook. I want to share with the reader a few paragraphs from my medical records.

CHIEF COMPLAINT AND HISTORY OF PRESENT ILLNESS:

The patient is a 20-year-old single white female who came into the E.R. several nights prior to admission in an agitated state. She was preoccupied with delusions that she had about her neighbor. She gave a history of having been fairly depressed with high anxiety for at least the past three years, and she had experienced frequent panic attacks and anxiety to the extent that she had not been able to hold down jobs. She stated that her spirits had been low fairly continually during the past three years and that she had had frequent suicidal thoughts which she had never acted upon. She had an interest in her neighbor, Bob, throughout much of this time, but apparently became delusional about him about nine months prior to admission when she apparently became quite certainly convinced that this married neighbor was in love with her, and that he was sending signals to her by the way that he would park his car or the way that he would close his curtains in his house. Her delusions began to extend to the point where she felt some kind of merger between her family and his family was evident. Her agitation surrounding these delusions had been steadily increasing and in the week prior to admission, she had stopped eating, and she was sleeping very little. She also began to fear that her own house had been bugged. Her mother brought her to the hospital on 9/19 and she was admitted on an Emergency Certificate. She began expressing paranoid thoughts about Dr. Smith, thinking the medication that she had been given had something "funny" in it.

MENTAL STATUS EXAMINATION:

In the E.R., the patient was alert and talked incessantly, often twisting her sunglasses. Her mood was depressed with positive suicidal ideations. She had inappropriate affect with frequent inappropriate smiling. Her speech was incessant and slightly pressured. Her thoughts were tangential. She had delusions regarding her next-door neighbor, and his involvement in her life. She had vague suicidal ideations, but no intent. She had no homicidal ideations. There was no evidence of hallucinations. On cognitive exam, she was oriented to person, place, and situation, but she was two days off in time. She had decreased attention span. Her short-term memory appeared to be intact, but her long-term memory was questionable.

HOSPITAL COURSE:

At the time of admission, the patient was very delusional, paranoid, and agitated. It was necessary to place her in lock and seclusion. On hospital day one, she was given a total of 35 mg of Haldol in divided doses, and she was given Moban 10 mg bid. She responded to this medication, and she had some softening of her delusions overnight. She tolerated the medication well except for some orthostatic hypotension. Because of her continual agitation on hospital day two, Ativan 2 mg bid was added. By the third day of hospitalization, she was able to be on the ward. She still had delusions, but she was not planning her life around them. The Haldol was decreased to 5 mg bid, and the Ativan was decreased to 1 mg bid. She remained on this with gradual improvement for several days. She continued to have problems with orthostatic hypotension and with tiredness. On 9/25/90, her Ativan was increased to 4 mg daily in divided doses and her Haldol was increased to 7 mg bid. At this time, by the following day, she had very little evidence of active psychosis. She obviously still had difficulty holding to her thoughts, but she realized that her thoughts regarding her next-door neighbor were delusional. She desired discharge, and this appeared to be a possibility.

Getting Your Medical Records

Everyone is entitled to have access to their medical records. I have copies of mine. Copies can cost as much as one dollar per page, but they are worth every penny.

First of all, you have to sign a release of information to get your medical records. Sometimes they charge you if you go over the limit of free copies. The reason you have to sign a release of information form is because no one can get your records without your permission. If anyone releases your medical records without your consent, it breaks the HIPPA Privacy Rule. (Google "HIPPA" if you have to file a complaint.) If you want to change something in your medical records, you have a right to amend them if you feel your health information is incorrect or incomplete. Your request for an amendment must be in writing, signed, and dated, and specify the record or records you wish to amend.

Also, the most important thing to know about getting medical records when you have a mental illness is that you can get everything except the physician's notes. Physician's notes are private notes and you need permission from your psychiatrist to gain access to them. When I inquired about this restriction, I was told by a medical records office worker that a patient killed herself after reading the notes taken by her psychiatrist. So, before they can be released, the attending psychiatrist must first determine if the patient can handle the material in the physician's notes.

What It's Like To Have Schizophrenia

As you might imagine, having schizophrenia is not fun. For the rest of my life, I have to go every month to get my blood drawn. If my white blood cell count is low, I must have it drawn once each week or every two weeks. If my white blood cell count is too low, I can't get my prescription. I have tried other drugs, but clozapine is the only drug that works for me. I never want to be hospitalized again, so I must always take my medication.

I see a psychiatrist once a month. I need twelve hours of sleep because the medication is very sedating. The medication makes me gain weight, so I have to exercise and watch what I eat. Those are the physical problems I experience with schizophrenia. The psychological and social problems center around the fact that some people are afraid of me when I tell them I have schizophrenia.

Understanding Voices

Every person I know with schizophrenia has heard voices, and I'm not talking about voices originating from a person sitting next to you, or voices conveyed over the telephone or some other communication device. I'm talking about voices that originate from a source that can only be heard by the individual with schizophrenia. I'm talking about auditory hallucinations, which are voices that originate within the psyche of the individual.

The voices can tell the individual to believe that which is truly unbelievable, or to believe that which is not true. Also, the voices can instruct the individual to do things that may be irrational, or even dangerous. For example, I remember my mother walking upstairs to check on me one night, and the voices told me that she had a knife and was coming to kill me. Of course, that was not true, but I was naturally very frightened and could have mistakenly taken defensive action against her.

In addition, I remember putting my hands in the air, simulating the strangulation of my grandmother. I felt I wanted to strangle her because the voices falsely accused her of ruining a relationship with my male neighbor. I yelled, "You ruined it! You ruined it!" However, the relationship was imaginary; it existed only inside my head, just as the voices existed only inside my head! So, even very trustworthy family members can be falsely described as untrustworthy or threatening by hallucinatory, accusatory voices.

Strangely enough, while the voices may originate from within the psyche of the individual, a person with schizophrenia may believe some voices originate from a television set or even a newspaper. Clearly, auditory hallucinations can be very disturbing and confusing because the individual cannot distinguish between what is real and what is not real. When you see people talking to themselves, you know they are responding to voices that no one else can hear. This is a classic symptom of schizophrenia!

Sometimes a person with schizophrenia may stay awake all night — and every night — for an extended period of time because they cannot turn off the internal voices. During a period when I was not taking any medication, I did not sleep for two weeks. I did not get even one hour of sleep during this period because relentless voices kept me awake. As one would expect, this led to my hospitalization.

Panic Disorder

Not only do I deal with schizophrenia, but I am also diagnosed with panic disorder. When I get a panic attack it is horrible. I feel dizzy, extremely nervous to be around people, my heart beats fast, and sometimes I feel like I will pass out. One time, I passed out in a line at McDonald's and had to have a family member pick me up there. Between the ages of 17 and 20 years old I was afraid to leave my house because of my panic disorder. The best way I can describe a panic attack is that you feel like everything is overwhelming; you feel like you are having a nervous breakdown. Sometimes when I have a panic attack I take lorazepam (Ativan), 5 mg, which has a tranquilizing effect on the central nervous system. I also go to Recovery, Inc. groups, which deal with panic and anxiety and are totally free. Go online to find a group near you if you suffer from panic attacks.

Schizophrenia And Street Drugs

From what I have read, street drugs can produce symptoms similar to schizophrenia. So, before a doctor can diagnose someone with schizophrenia, he or she needs to do a drug test first to make sure street drugs are not causing the symptoms. Dual diagnosis is the condition of having a drug or alcohol problem as well as a mental illness.

Schizophrenia And Smoking

During my lifetime I have been in contact with numerous people who have struggled with the disturbing symptoms associated with schizophrenia. Like many other people with some form of mental illness, a large number of people with schizophrenia have become addicted to nicotine and smoke cigarettes on a regular basis. From what I have observed, I would say that people with schizophrenia or some other form of mental illness are far more likely to smoke than people in the general population.

On page 273 of his book, *Surviving Schizophrenia: A Manual for Families, Patients, and Providers*, (5th Edition), E. Fuller Torrey, M.D. stated that "Nicotine reduces anxiety, reduces sedation, and improves concentration in some people, which might be a form of self-medication for the person with schizophrenia." Because people with schizophrenia and other types of mental problems experience very stressful symptoms such as auditory or visual hallucinations, the habit of smoking may be perceived as helping relieve stress induced by these and other disturbing symptoms, however smoking contributes to a vast array of health problems.

For people who have become addicted to smoking, whether or not they are suffering from some form of mental illness, I recommend the book *How I Quit Smoking in 31 Days After Smoking for 32 Years*. In this book the author, Michael T. Petro, Jr., describes in detail how he quit smoking and says anyone can do so by following his simple but effective plan. I'm glad I never started smoking!

Suicide And Schizophrenia

According to the NAMI (National Alliance on Mental Illness) Greater Cleveland website, 90 percent of the people who die through suicide have been diagnosed with some form of mental illness.

People diagnosed with schizophrenia must take prescription medication. Without medication, suicide is seen as an option far too often. Sometimes, though, even people on medication commit suicide. For example, when I was in Dr. Herbert Meltzer's clozapine study, I became friends with a girl named Julie who also had schizophrenia. I don't know if she was taking her medication or not. I do know she would throw parties when her parents weren't home, and she would smoke pot and drink beer. I never joined the party people when they did that stuff. Shortly after one party, I had a routine session with my psychiatrist. "Have you seen Julie?" he asked me. I said "No," and he responded by saying that Julie shot herself in the head with a gun. I was shocked and devastated. I felt so sorry for her family.

I also had a brush with suicide before I was diagnosed with schizophrenia. From age 17 to age 20, I was depressed. I was so miserable I wanted to kill myself. I did go as far as to call the

National Suicide Prevention Lifeline. Their telephone number is 1-800-273-8255. I don't remember the details of what we discussed, but I do remember that the call helped. According to JAMA Psychiatry, the drug clozapine reduces the risk of suicide. There is always help for any problem. Today, medications are far more effective in alleviating depression and suicidal thoughts than what we had in the past. If you are having suicidal thoughts, then it is time to get help. Do not isolate yourself. Suicidal thoughts are not accurate reflections of reality. Most importantly, keep in mind that suicide is a permanent solution to a temporary problem. It is a permanent solution to a temporary state of mind, therefore it is the wrong solution.

Violence And Schizophrenia

In 2006 I had a terrifying experience. I have been a member of NAMI (National Alliance on Mental Illness) for years, and I have associated with other members of this helpful organization. Two of my associates were a guy named Albert and a girl named Lisa. I frequently told Albert that I thought Lisa's medication wasn't working, or that she wasn't taking her medication.

On March 23, 2006, when a NAMI meeting was over, I went outside to talk to other members. Lisa came up to me and asked, "Are we going to the bar tonight?" I told her, "No, we are going to the bookstore." Lisa became very angry and said, "Why do you like books, bitch?" I said, "I don't know." She then pushed me and tried to grab me. Terrified, I started running toward Nicole, the group leader, who was sitting in her car. I yelled, "Let me in!" Nicole let me in and locked the car door. Lisa came up to the car door, pounded on the window, and said, "I am going to kill you...you bitch."

Nicole started to drive off with me in her car, but Lisa got into her own car and pulled right next to Nicole's car. She gave us the finger, and then drove off. I reported this to the police, who said they would call her mental health agency and have her evaluated. One of the other NAMI members told me that Lisa was hearing voices that night. As discussed in the previous section titled "Understanding Voices," hearing voices is a classic symptom of schizophrenia. Albert had tried to tell Lisa's case worker and parents a long time ago that she wasn't behaving appropriately, but no one listened.

With schizophrenia, people can become violent if they don't receive the proper help, and schizophrenia is the most severe of all the mental illnesses because those who have it are not in touch with reality. When those with schizophrenia find a drug that works for them, they become stabilized. Once stabilized on medication, they can look back and remember some of the crazy thoughts they had and some of the crazy things they did. With or without medication, memory is retained, but with medication individuals with schizophrenia can look back and gain insight into how they behave when they are not taking their medication.

Schizophrenia And The Police

NAMI Greater Cleveland is trying to work with law enforcement officers so they can receive CIT (Crisis Intervention Training). By receiving this specialized form of training, they would be better equipped to deal with individuals who are struggling with mental illness. You can ask for a CIT-trained police officer if you have to call the police.

Doctors

People suffering from mental illness often find it necessary to change doctors. I have seen several psychiatrists since I was diagnosed with schizophrenia. Some of these doctors were not very impressive. For example, one doctor actually ate lunch while talking to me. Another wanted to change my meds although she knew the medication I was taking was working well for me. Two doctors I saw while looking for a new psychiatrist (and was stabilized on meds) told me I needed to be re-diagnosed. If they were helpful doctors, they would have evaluated me by interviewing me and some of my family members. They could have at least reviewed my medical records, not just see me for five minutes and tell me I need to be re-diagnosed. They seemed to base their decisions on very little evidence.

Remember the question, "What is a schizophrenic supposed to look like?" I have found there are a lot of psychiatrists who do not specialize in schizophrenia. It's important to find a psychiatrist who does. I also recommend finding a psychiatrist who works out of a hospital in case you need to be hospitalized.

Also, it should be noted that a psychiatrist is a physician and therefore can prescribe medication; however, a psychologist is not a physician and consequently is limited to nonmedical psychotherapy. This is important because therapists cannot talk schizophrenics out of their biochemically-based symptoms; only medication can control such symptoms. A psychologist's talk therapy can be effective, but only after the individual has been stabilized on medication.

A psychiatrist I was seeing for five years died suddenly. This was certainly a devastating shock for his family and friends, but it was also very unfortunate for me, and perhaps for all his patients. He was always willing to see me when I had a problem; he made sure I was doing well on my medication, and he never tried to change my medication because he knew it was working well for me. He also listened to my problems and prescribed extra meds when I had terrible panic attacks. He served as an example of how a truly good psychiatrist should behave toward his or her patients.

I have changed psychiatrists several times because I was often not satisfied or sure they were a good fit for me.

Forensic Psychiatry

What is a forensic psychiatrist? What is a forensic patient? A forensic psychiatrist is a medical doctor who is trained in both law and mental health, and works with people who have psychiatric problems, such as schizophrenia. Forensic patients are those who have been accused of a crime and found unsuitable to stand trial because of a mental illness. Forensic patients are also those people who have been tried and found not guilty due to mental illness.

Medication

Due to variations in body chemistry, medication that may work for one person may not work for another. Also, the time it takes for a given medicine to work varies from one person to another. In my own experience, it took three months for clozapine to work properly. Antipsychotic medications such as clozapine are for people with serious mental health problems, such as schizophrenia. They work by affecting dopamine in the brain. The newer antipsychotics are called atypical, while the older antipsychotics are called conventional. Unlike many other drugs, anti-psychotics are not addictive. They may work in a few days, but usually take several weeks before positive results are observed.

I have tried conventional drugs such as haloperidol (Haldol), loxapine (Loxitane), and many others. As stated earlier, I am now on the atypical antipsychotic drug clozapine. Clozapine is used to treat severe schizophrenia symptoms in people who have not responded well to other medications. Clozapine can cause agranulocytosis, which is a decrease in the number of white blood cells. Due to this side effect, patients who take clozapine will have their blood levels tested every two weeks for the first six months of treatment. After that, it can be tested on a monthly basis.

Some medications can cause tardive dyskinesia when used long-term. This is a condition similar to Tourette syndrome wherein the patient experiences uncontrolled muscle movements. When taking the drug haloperidol one of my arms would move up and down involuntarily. I have a friend who fumbles his fingers involuntarily as a result of treatment with antipsychotic drugs. This movement disorder may develop months, years, or perhaps many decades after taking certain antipsychotic medications. Unfortunately, there is no known cure for tardive dyskinesia. That's why it's important to identify the symptoms as soon as possible. Lowering the dose or switching to another medication may be necessary when symptoms are observed. Fortunately for me and many other people with schizophrenia, tardive dyskinesia is not known to be a side effect of clozapine.

When I first started taking clozapine for Dr. Herbert Meltzer's study, I was put on 200 mg doses. With that dosage I needed only five to six hours of sleep each night. When the study was over, they took me off clozapine and I ended up in the hospital. They stabilized me after three months, and increased my dosage of clozapine to 350 mg. With this dosage I now need 12 hours of sleep. The higher the dose, the more sedation!

It is common for those with schizophrenia to think they are not ill, and thus believe they have no need for antipsychotic medication. But I know that for the rest of my life I will take my medicine, because I never want to be hospitalized again. I dread feeling imprisoned. In reality though, the hospital stabilized me, so I guess I should not complain. Some state laws say a person cannot be forced to take medication, but I feel that individuals with schizophrenia should be required to take medication because they could be a danger to themselves or others. Also, when people are initially discharged from a hospital, someone has to make sure they take their medication in order to prevent a relapse.

For those who do not have insurance to pay for medication, there are patient assistance programs that can be very helpful. For example, some patients who meet certain eligibility requirements set by drug companies may actually receive free prescription drugs. It is very important to have a good relationship with your pharmacist as well. A good pharmacist can answer questions about side effects, drug interactions, and can tell you exactly how to take your medicine and what to do if you miss a dose or take it incorrectly. I am very pleased with the pharmacy I go to and wouldn't go anywhere else.

The number one reason people do not take medicine is the fear of side effects. I have been on many drugs with side effects, for example, one drug gave me weird movements, one made me lie in bed all day, and one gave me blurred vision. The only side effects for the one I am on now are drooling at night, heavy sedation, and weight gain. But with schizophrenia you must take medication because that is the only thing that can control your intrusive thoughts. Nothing else will work! The side effects I experience from the medication are nothing compared to the symptoms of schizophrenia, such as paranoia. I will take medicine for the rest of my life.

Schizophrenia And Drug Interactions

People who are taking prescription drugs of any type must pay close attention to possible drug interactions. From what I have read, clozapine, the drug I am currently taking, can interact with caffeine and lower one's white blood cell count and increase side effects. Caffeine, which is a stimulant drug, can be found in many sodas, teas, energy drinks, coffee, and chocolate — especially dark chocolate. A good caffeine-free alternative to chocolate is carob; it tastes like chocolate, but without the caffeine!

When I drink caffeinated green tea before bedtime I toss and turn for hours. Drinks with alcohol make me immediately dizzy, so I never consume alcoholic beverages. Lastly, from what I have read, smoking can also lower one's white blood cell count. For this reason I encourage others not to smoke.

Nutrition And Health

Nutrition is extremely important for people who have schizophrenia because we are on medication for life. By eating right we can enjoy a healthy life. Unfortunately, the medicine clozapine can cause agranulocytosis, which, as stated earlier, is a low white blood cell count. Currently, I am following the Blood Type A food, beverage, and supplement lists from *Eat Right for Your Type* by Peter J. D'Adamo, M.D. (Berkeley Books, 2002). On page five of this book Dr. D'Adamo says, "When you eat the foods from your blood type the highly beneficial foods act as a medicine, the neutral foods act like a food, and the avoid foods act like a poison in your body." If it were not for the Blood Type diet, my blood counts would be really low.

According to medical science, there are four different blood types, which include O, A, B, and AB. For more information regarding the types of diets recommended for the four different blood types, the reader is encouraged to go to the website, *www.4YourType.com*, and check out the information provided.

My blood type is A+, and these are some of the things that I swear raise my white blood cell count: molasses on plain yogurt, aloe vera drinks, carrot juice, and decaffeinated green tea. I consume absolutely no artificial sweeteners and no alcohol; they always lower my white blood cell count. Your body pH is another factor to consider in maintaining good overall health. You can monitor your pH, or the degree to which your body is acidic or alkaline, by testing your urine with pH strips that can be purchased online. At the website *www.drdavidwilliams.com*, it is stated that, to prevent disease, the human body should be slightly alkaline. To make your body more alkaline, go online and Google "alkaline foods" and choose the correct foods for your blood type.

Here are some health tips I have learned:

1. A good carbohydrate will have the word "whole" on the food label. If it does not say "whole," it is not a healthy carb.

2. Sodium should not be higher than calories.

3. I never buy anything with high fructose corn syrup. It can be in breads, cereals, yogurts, and beverages, so read labels.

4. I never buy anything with hydrogenated oils. They clog arteries and so do foods with lots of oil in them. Read labels.

5. Foods that raise cholesterol are roasted nuts (look for raw instead) and cheese. When I overeat cheese, I gain weight quickly because it is a high-fat food.

6. If you are going to eat hot dogs or lunch meat, look on the label for meats without nitrates.

7. If you eat bread, sprouted breads are healthier. Try Ezekiel bread!

Many people with schizophrenia live on a restricted income, and not by choice. Buying a sufficient amount of healthy food can be a struggle. To buy healthy foods more cheaply, Whole Foods has their own organic brand called 365 with great prices. Giant Eagle also has their own organic brand called Nature's Basket. Trader Joe's and Wal-Mart are loaded with inexpensive organic foods.

I used to take Omega-3 supplements because doctors claim they are good for the brain. I noticed that when I took fish oil supplements every morning, I would get constant burping and indigestion. I went online to see if fish oil supplements can cause indigestion or acid reflux, and I discovered that they can. They may not cause acid reflux in everyone, but for me they did. I also asked a pharmacist and he told me that clozapine can cause acid reflux, so he said not to take fish oil because the acid reflux will be worse than the benefits provided by the fish oil. Consequently, I no longer take fish oil supplements. I try to get my Omega-3 through diet. Some foods I eat for Omega-3 are salmon, walnuts, chia seeds, and Omega-3 eggs. Unfortunately, tomatoes give me acid reflux, but I still occasionally eat food containing tomatoes!

I also want to mention the most commonly recognized allergen foods: gluten, dairy, corn, eggs, soy, peanuts, and night shade vegetables (tomatoes, bell peppers, potatoes, and eggplant). I still eat many of these foods but I am just letting you know which foods could cause an allergic reaction. The one allergen food that I occasionally eat is soy. There is controversy over whether or not soy is good for you. Therefore, if I do eat soy, it must be organic!

In March 2015, I went to a holistic nutritionist. By looking at my eyes she could tell I had Candida, also called Candida albicans. Candida is a yeast that grows naturally in the intestines.

Prescription medications can destroy the friendly bacteria in your intestines, causing an overgrowth of Candida yeast.

Candida yeast overgrowth may also be caused by too much sugar in the diet. The Candida diet is a sugar-free diet and I do not mean eating sugar-free sweeteners. I mean eliminating sugar and all other sweeteners from your diet! The holistic nutritionist told me to add coconut oil to my diet because it contains caprylic acid, which helps to reduce Candida yeast. She also highly recommended a gluten-free diet. There is much controversy over whether wheat gluten is a contributing factor in schizophrenia. I was allergic to wheat as a child, so it could be true. Eating gluten-free, from what I have read, may reduce the symptoms of schizophrenia.

Almost every person I know on medication for a mental illness has a bloated stomach, which I believe is caused by prescription medication. Remember, Candida is a yeast overgrowth problem. If you make bread and add yeast, the bread rises! I believe the yeast growth caused by prescriptions drugs can bloat the stomach. So, to combat this side effect I take probiotic supplements and eat foods containing probiotics such as yogurt, kefir, and sour cream!

Perhaps most importantly, probiotics have never reduced my white blood cell counts; instead, they have actually made them go up. I also believe probiotics have helped prevent me from getting the stomach flu.

According to many reputable websites (including that of the U.S. Food and Drug Administration), some prescription drugs may have a toxic effect on the liver. So to cleanse my liver, I squeeze a little lemon juice in a glass of water before drinking it. In addition to detoxifying the liver, this simple formula can also be used to improve digestion.

For those living in the Northeastern Ohio area who are searching for someone to guide them through natural forms of therapy, I recommend Dr. Jane Semple, M.A., N.D. This naturopathic doctor operates the Alternative Healing Institute located at 4965 Dover Center Road in North Olmstead, Ohio. Her telephone number is 440-777-2665. She has been very helpful in guiding me through the choices I have made regarding natural approaches to health care.

Supplements

I am not a physician, so I am not offering medical advice here or anywhere else in this book; instead, I am simply providing the reader with what I have learned over the years regarding supplements and drug interactions. If you are taking any type of medication always consult with your doctor before taking any supplements. This is vital because some supplements may interact with your medication and cause undesirable side effects. Also, keep in mind that what works for me may not work for you because my body chemistry may be very different from yours.

I take a multivitamin and Vitamin D3. My doctor said my body chemistry was low in Vitamin D3, so I take 1,000 IU each day. I have found that taking Vitamin D3 helps reduce my anxiety level and also eases depression.

Recipes

I have assembled a variety of recipes. I have found that each of the recipes below produces foods that are both nutritious and delicious. I hope you enjoy them as much as I do.

Tofu Chocolate Mousse

- 12 oz. soft tofu, drained
- ¼ cup cacao powder
- ⅓ cup maple syrup
- 1 tablespoon instant coffee granules

Process tofu, cacao powder, maple syrup, and coffee granules in a food processor or blender until smooth. Eat right away, or refrigerate overnight. It tastes like pudding.

Tofu with Almond Butter Sauce

- 1 package of extra firm tofu
- ¼ cup almond butter
- ¼ cup water
- 1-2 tablespoons honey

Slice and warm tofu. Pour almond sauce over tofu. Enjoy!

Zucchini Soup

- 1 carton of vegetable broth
- 4-5 zucchinis, sliced with the skin intact

Bring broth to a boil. Add zucchini and boil until the zucchini is soft. Cool. Blend in blender until it looks like soup. Reheat and enjoy!

Tofu Chili

- 1 package of pumpkin soup
- 3 cans of beans, any kind, drained
- 1 cup of chopped celery
- Package extra firm tofu (16 oz.), cut into bite-size pieces
- Sour cream (optional)

Combine pumpkin soup, beans, celery, and tofu. Bring to a boil. When heated add sour cream if desired, and enjoy!

Mashed Cauliflower

- 1 bag frozen cauliflower
- 3 tablespoons butter
- ¼ cup of milk

Add to boiling water and boil until soft. Drain, then add milk and butter. Mash and enjoy!

Avocado Smoothie

- ½ avocado
- 1 cup unsweetened almond milk
- 1 teaspoon raw honey
- 2 teaspoons chia seeds
- 1 teaspoon cinnamon

Blend. Makes one serving. Enjoy!

Deviled Avocado Eggs

- 1 whole avocado
- 12 eggs
- Mayonnaise (as much as you want)

Hard boil eggs. Cool and cut eggs in half; take out yolks, set them aside. Mix avocado with egg yolks and mayonnaise. Put mixture into egg whites. Enjoy!

Hot Chocolate (Serves 2)

- 2 cups milk
- ¼ cup cacao powder
- 1 teaspoon molasses
- 1 teaspoon ground cinnamon
- ½ teaspoon vanilla extract

Add all ingredients in a small saucepan. Whisk over medium heat until cacao powder is incorporated and mixture is hot, about five minutes. Be sure not to let the milk scald.

Fitness And Medication

Before I was diagnosed with schizophrenia, I was always thin and could never gain weight. In 10th grade, I weighed 95 pounds. I would eat a lot of food but would never gain weight. However, when I was taking the drug Haldol, I went from 115 to 180 pounds. I believe the weight gain occurred because while taking Haldol, I would lie in bed all day and only get up to eat. When I was switched to clozapine, I no longer spent the day in bed. But even on clozapine I have gained weight. So, I walk to stay slim. I try to walk two miles five days per week. In the past, I joined a free group called Food Addicts Anonymous, a group that deals with people who have food issues. Google "Food Addicts Anonymous" to find a group in your area.

Grooming And Schizophrenia

While many women (and men) with schizophrenia are well-groomed, many others are not. There was a time I wouldn't shower because I thought people could see me while I was in the shower. Therefore, not showering or not bathing could be a sign of schizophrenia. There is a girl at the mall who is very well groomed, but she talks to herself without head phones. Once again I repeat the question, what is a schizophrenic supposed to look like?

Dating And Schizophrenia

Although I have never checked out these websites myself, there are two websites for people with a mental illness who would like to try dating. The two sites are as follows: *www.trueacceptance.com* and *www.nolongerlonely.com*.

People May Use Your Illness Against You

I tried to break up in a nice way with one boyfriend, but he continued to show up at places I visited, and he would also e-mail me. I started to get angry about it, so I sent him an e-mail saying I was planning to get a restraining order if he didn't leave me alone. He e-mailed me back that he had already told the police about my condition. After reading that e-mail, I cried. He tried to make me look unstable by bringing my mental illness into the situation, when all I wanted to do was break up with him.

His father, who is an optometrist and not a psychiatrist, would constantly tell me that I didn't have schizophrenia. Again, what is a schizophrenic supposed to look like?

Stigma And Discrimination

I had severe ear popping and went to several ear doctors. None of them could figure out the cause of this problem. One of the doctors said the ear popping was normal, though severe ear popping to me is not normal. I eventually saw a TMJ (temporomandibular joint disorder) specialist, whom my dentist recommended. He said it was TMJ and sold me mouth splints, which did nothing. I fought that case and got my money back.

When I went to an ear doctor at a local hospital, I was asked what medications I was taking. I said I was taking clozapine for schizophrenia, and I feel they discriminated against me based upon my response. I got copies of my medical records from the ear doctors to read what they said about me, and they kept mentioning "paranoid schizophrenia." One of the ear doctors said to my face, "I don't mean to call you crazy, but this problem is in your head!" He also asked me right out, "What is your diagnosis?" (He already knew my diagnosis because he put it in my records.) I answered him by asking, "What does my diagnosis have to do with my ear problem?" He answered, "Everything."

This worried me because these doctors were talking more about my diagnosis than they were about my ear problem. He conducted a pressure test and found excessive pressure in both ears. He said he could insert tubes in my ears to relieve the excessive pressure, but I was so humiliated by what he said that I would not allow him to do so. I cried when I left the doctor's office. I silently asked myself, "Who cries when leaving a doctor's office after seeking help?" Later, I allowed another ear doctor to put tubes in my ears to relieve the excessive pressure. This was the only treatment that improved my ear popping problem.

I have a psychiatrist who I see once a month. So, why would I go to an ear doctor for a psychiatric problem, or vice versa? This upset me so much that I went to the hospital's ombudsman office. Basically that did nothing but make me upset once again. The ombudsman sent me a letter in the mail in response to my concerns.

In the letter the ombudsman noted that I had "expressed concerns" about an unpleasant interaction with one of their physicians. She acknowledged that my main concern was that Dr. X (of course, that's not his real name) seemed to concentrate more on my mental illness than on my ear problem.

The ombudsman said that she shared my concerns with Dr. X directly, and Dr. X "apologizes for your concern." The ombudsman said Dr. X wanted to explain how my mental illness may "play a role in other medical conditions." My concern about Dr. X had been recorded, and sorrow was expressed about my dissatisfaction with the services I had received. The letter ended with a "Thank you" from the ombudsman, and it was further stated that they "continuously strive to improve" their services and are "grateful" I shared my experience with them.

The ombudsman office is supposed to help you if you have a problem with a medical service, if you have questions about the care you received, if you have concerns about any employees, if the health care facility did not provide satisfactory service during inpatient or outpatient care, or if you have a billing complaint related to your medical care.

Based on my experiences in dealing with doctors and others, I learned that just about anyone can discriminate against a person who has received the diagnosis of schizophrenia. No matter who he or she may be dealing with, if there is a conflict or a misunderstanding, the person with schizophrenia will always be viewed as "the wrong one," and will therefore be seen as the source of the problem. So, it is much more difficult for people who have schizophrenia to defend their point of view or their rights because they are assumed to be the cause of any conflict or misunderstanding. While this can be very frustrating, it is worsened by the fact that I have known so-called "normal" people who don't act as normal as me when I am on my medication and quite stable. However, these "normal" people are still less likely than a person with schizophrenia to be the victim of discrimination.

Schizophrenia And The Workplace

The Americans with Disabilities Act (ADA) protects disabled people's rights in the workplace. If you have been discriminated against while trying to get a job or while on the job, you need to contact a civil rights attorney.

Volunteering On The Mental Ward

The most rewarding thing I do is volunteering on the mental ward at a local hospital, where I promote NAMI Greater Cleveland. The patients really appreciate me. Here are some of the things I have learned from volunteering:

1. Some of these patients have never heard of NAMI.
2. They usually do not want to admit they have a mental illness.
3. They usually believe they do not need medication.

What Is A Schizophrenic Supposed To Look Like?

4. Some patients are very ill. They look normal on the outside, but when they speak, you can tell they are very ill. For example, one man with schizophrenia said to me, "I know how I got schizophrenia — a roach was on my birthday cake!" And there was a woman who said, "Someone transplanted my brain."

5. Some patients stay in the hospital for a while, and some come and go more quickly. In 2017, hospitals don't keep patients as long as they used to, probably due to their insurance requirements. That is not a good thing. Because of this, it is possible that people will leave the hospital before they are properly stabilized.

Where To Go For Psychiatric Help In The Cleveland, Ohio Area!

Saint Vincent Charity Hospital And Medical Center

Although I have never been a patient at Saint Vincent Charity Hospital and Medical Center, through my research I have concluded that it may offer the very best psychiatric care in the Cleveland, Ohio area. Their Psychiatric Emergency Department is operational 24/7, and it is one of only two hospitals in Ohio that offers such around-the-clock psychiatric emergency care. This facility is known throughout the region for its expertise in behavioral health, and is staffed with psychiatrists, psychiatric nurses, social workers, and mental health technicians. Inpatient services include the following: comprehensive assessment, crisis intervention, occupational therapy, recreational therapy, chemical dependency treatment, medication management, psycho-educational groups and individual interactions, and patient and family education. Psychiatric care as well as alcohol and other drug dependency care are also provided through outpatient services. Lastly, Saint Vincent Charity Hospital and Medical Center offers geropsychiatric services for older adults experiencing memory loss, dementia, and other mental health problems.

University Hospitals Connor Integrative Health Network

Those with mental health problems may wish to explore a specialty called "integrative psychiatry," offered by University Hospitals of Cleveland, Ohio. At their website, the visitor discovers that the University Hospitals Connor Integrative Health Network "offers integrative psychiatry to enable patients to get in touch with and engage the body's natural healing abilities. This holistic mind-body therapy is designed to enhance the whole person and it benefits patients with [a variety of] conditions." Anxiety, chronic pain, depression, insomnia, fatigue, and stress-related problems are listed as conditions that may be addressed with integrative psychiatry.

At their website it is noted that integrative psychiatry "moves beyond medications," and is offered as a "holistic therapy." This form of therapy is based on the logical notion that one's mental health is impacted by many interconnected factors such as one's biology, environment, beliefs, family dynamics, and constitution. Yoga, guided imagery, talk therapy, and massage and meditation are among the "mind-body treatments" that "move beyond medication and diagnoses, and emphasize the healing power within."

As one who has experienced a variety of treatments over the years, I am intrigued by the natural approach outlined for integrative psychiatry. However, while treatments other than medication may be beneficial, based on my personal experience I believe that medication is central to any treatment plan designed for people struggling with schizophrenia.

The web address that will take you directly to the webpage containing the above information and numerous informative links is as follows:

> http://www.uhconnorintegrativehealth.org/services/integrative-psychiatry.

To schedule an integrative psychiatry appointment one is directed to call 216-285-4070.

Additional Support Services

Magnolia Clubhouse In Cleveland, Ohio

When I first got out of the hospital in 1990, I went to a place called Hill House. Today, it is called Magnolia Clubhouse. Just recently, in 2015, I decided to go to Magnolia Clubhouse with a friend from the NAMI group to check it out. I discovered they provide lunch from 12:00 p.m. to 1:00 p.m. To become a member, you must have a mental illness, fill out a brief application, and pay one dollar per day if you decide to go. They have self-improvement activities and can help you find employment, doctor services, and housing. One thing I observed at Magnolia Clubhouse was the Health Group held Wednesdays at 2:00 p.m. It appears to me that mentally ill people really need help with nutrition and health. This is a great resource, because I have noticed that many mentally ill people are overweight.

Overall, I was very impressed and I plan to return. While there, I met a social worker who attended high school with me. She said that she could tell something was wrong with me in high school, but she could not identify a specific problem. She said I looked very sad and depressed. She told me her father had paranoid schizophrenia.

Social workers are trained professionals who may offer counseling, psychotherapy, or assistance with managing the complexities of the mental health system. Social workers may also be called "case managers."

NAMI Greater Cleveland

NAMI, the National Alliance on Mental Illness, is a great resource for people with mental health challenges. Group meetings are available for people with mental illness, as well as for their family members and other caregivers. The general public is also welcome to attend community education meetings hosted by mental health professionals. For only $3.00 one can become a member of NAMI and receive newsletters such as *NAMI Voice* and *News Briefs,* and the magazine titled, *Advocate*. Google "NAMI" to locate numerous informative websites.

Movies About Schizophrenia You Should Consider Watching

Canvas: This movie is a true story of a mother who struggled with schizophrenia. I loved this movie! It really shows how people with schizophrenia can act when not taking medicine or realizing they have a problem. At *www.HealthCentral.com*, I found the following movie critique: "It is a rare event when a motion picture presents paranoid schizophrenia in a responsible and accurate light...The movie is a remarkably honest and unembellished account of a father and a ten-year-old son's firsthand experiences with a mother attempting to cope with schizophrenia, a mother who loves both of them dearly despite her illness." Robin Cunningham, who wrote the critique of *Canvas*, said this movie was "exceptionally well done." He further stated that it could "play an important role in fighting mental health stigma."

A Beautiful Mind: A friend from my high school once told me that I said there was fire coming out of my drawers. Of course, there really was no fire there. So, people struggling with schizophrenia see things that aren't really there, and this movie provides excellent examples of how they experience visual and auditory hallucinations. It also demonstrates in a very instructional way how they have great difficulty distinguishing, for example, imaginary characters from real people.

A Beautiful Mind is based on a true story. It covers the life of John Nash, who suffered from the classical symptoms of schizophrenia. Nash was a mathematical genius who taught at Princeton University. In spite of his mental illness, in 1994 he won the Nobel

Memorial Prize in Economic Sciences. He also received the Abel Prize, which is considered to be one of the most prestigious honors one can receive in the field of mathematics. John Nash was a gifted mathematician who excelled despite his schizophrenia. The entire movie is available for free at several sites online.

The Soloist: This movie is about a black man, Nathaniel Anthony Ayers, who was a Julliard College dropout. (Once when I went to Magnolia Clubhouse, one of the workers there told me that Nathaniel used to play his cello right on a corner near Magnolia Avenue!) Nathaniel dropped out of school and became homeless as a result of his struggle with schizophrenia. The movie shows how this gifted musician survived on the mean streets of Los Angeles. That is where Nathaniel meets Steve Lopez, a *Los Angeles Times* columnist. Steve tries to help Nathaniel by getting him an apartment through a mental health agency called LAMP.

I liked this movie, but I didn't agree with one comment made by the guy who played the part of the LAMP employee. He said, "Nathaniel doesn't need one more person telling him he needs medication." I disagree. I think any mental health agency should promote medication, because people with schizophrenia cannot recognize that they have a problem. In this movie, Nathaniel didn't think he needed medication. I hope to this day that Nathaniel is doing well. Everyone with schizophrenia should be encouraged to find the proper medication through his or her doctor.

Love & Mercy: In 2015 the movie *Love & Mercy* was released. This is a very informative movie about the life of Brian Wilson, a songwriter and cofounder of the Beach Boys. Unknown to many Americans, this gifted individual was diagnosed with paranoid schizophrenia, and he faced all the challenges that others have had to endure when given this potentially debilitating diagnosis. But despite his illness, he overcame very difficult hardships and helped make the Beach Boys an extremely popular and successful musical group.

The story of the life of Brian Wilson — as told in *Love & Mercy* — serves as an inspiration to all who are faced with any sort of serious challenge. Whether you are forced to deal with psychological problems, financial problems, marital problems, physical problems, or whatever, this movie can inspire the viewer with the courage needed to face and overcome any and all of life's challenges.

Not only did Brian Wilson have to battle the voices in his head, he also had to deal with the misguided voice and counter-productive behavior of his therapist. His over-controlling therapist, as depicted in this movie, may have done more harm than good in his interactions with his patient, Brian Wilson. What everyone can learn from this film is that choice of a therapist is critical, and must not be taken lightly. Try to find a therapist you like, who shows you compassion, and whose therapeutic style works for you.

Love & Mercy is an outstanding movie, and should be viewed by all mental health professionals, students, patients, and their family members! I watched it, enjoyed it, learned from it, and was inspired by it! I hope it will do the same for you!

Reading Material About Schizophrenia You Should Consider Reviewing

I recommend three books: *To Cry a Dry Tear*, by Bill McPhee; *The Quiet Room*, by Lori Schiller; and *Surviving Schizophrenia*, by E. Fuller Torrey, M.D. I also recommend an article in the February, 2016 issue of *Reader's Digest* titled, *What It's Like To Be A Person With Schizophrenia*.

Dr. Lillian Glass, a psychologist, is reportedly a "body language expert," and has appeared on many television shows to analyze the body language of others, especially celebrities. Dr. Glass has appeared on programs such as *Dr. Phil, Nicole Grace, The Insider, Entertainment Tonight,* and other popular television programs. She has also authored many books, such as *The Body Language of Liars, Toxic Men, Toxic People*, and many others.

In reading Dr. Glass's book, *Toxic People*, I found that I was disappointed by the manner in which she describes what she refers to as the "mental case." You may wish to read this book to see if you agree with me.

Group Homes And Housing

Not all mentally ill people can take good care of themselves. Some need to live in a group home. I have a friend who went to my old clinic. Her father put her in a group home after her mother died. She hates it. She says she has no freedom, strict rules, and has to wake up early for her medication and breakfast. She also told me that the group home owner is mean. Almost every time my mom and I call to take her out, the group home owner will not let her go. We don't understand why!

I have another friend who lives in a group home, and this is what he told me: "You can have a roommate or a private room. Some residents are high-functioning (meaning they can drive) and some are low-functioning. Sometimes the food is horrible." This concerns me because people on meds need to eat healthy foods. He also said, "Someone does the cleaning and laundry for you. No activities! There is a curfew of 9:00 p.m. Sometimes they will call the police if you leave without signing out. Most residents go to bed at 9:00 p.m. and wake up at 7:00 a.m. to take meds, but you can go back to bed. Medications are delivered to the group home. You have to take the bus or drive to your doctor's appointments, and there are no visitors."

My mother told me that before they released me from the hospital, they told her she should consider putting me in a group home. She said the only way she would consider it was if she could visit a group home herself to see what it was like. When she visited one, she thought that the people there were walking around like zombies, and she would never consider putting me there. My mom is not even sure who checks these group homes to see how well they take care of the residents.

My Mom's Advice To Other Mothers

My mom says that the best advice she can give other mothers is that you have to be patient. It takes time to find the right medicine, and once found, it takes time for the medicine to work. She told me some of the meds I was taking didn't work. Some worsened my condition and she would get frustrated with the doctors. She also says that being the mother of someone who has schizophrenia can be scary. For example, if the meds are not working right and you don't get help for that family member, it is possible they can harm you or themselves. No one else knows what their thoughts are, or what the voices are telling them to do.

Based on her observation of my behavior over a period of many years, she says the number one thing you shouldn't do is force family members to do things if you want them to get better. Most often, persuasion produces far better results than force. She also says people with schizophrenia need a lot of rest, so let them get enough sleep and don't label them as lazy or unmotivated!

Denial

Sometimes mentally ill people are in denial that they have schizophrenia and they don't want to accept their diagnosis; sometimes family members are in denial and they might say things like, "Oh, just snap out of it!" With schizophrenia, you cannot just snap out of it. Also, no one causes it, it is a chemical imbalance in the brain.

How To Avoid Relapse

First and foremost, accept the fact that you have an illness. Secondly, do not stop taking your medication because you feel better. You are feeling better precisely because you are taking your medication as prescribed by your doctor! Lastly, keep in mind that poor grooming, lack of motivation, self-isolation, and poor sleeping are all signs of relapse!

Schizophrenia And God

Oftentimes schizophrenia can cause religious delusions. When I was cleaning a drawer one day, I found something I wrote on a piece of paper. It mentioned weird religious experiences. Here is what I wrote:

Felt like the devil was going to kill me. I panicked and read the Bible. Felt like Jesus' spirit was inside my mind. Felt like Jesus was giving psychic messages. I thought my black cat was the devil and wanted to squirt her with water thinking it was holy water.

When hospitalized I thought I was Jesus. I was afraid of evil spirits and had to sleep with the light on. In spite of these delusions, I am religious and I do believe in God.

I believe God wanted this book to be written. I always attended a church that had a 7:07 p.m. evening service, and just as I started writing the manuscript for this book, the number 707 showed up everywhere. I have seen it on receipts, medical statements, phone numbers, addresses, and license plates. Once I was sitting in a writers' group and a phone number with the area code 707 appeared on my phone. It was a wrong number, but it still contained the number 707! Even the United States Copyright Office had a 707 area code. Lastly, sometimes when I check a clock or my watch the time displayed will be 7:07. I find this phenomenon unexplainable and unique to me!

So, What Is A Schizophrenic Supposed To Look Like?

How do we answer the question, "What is a schizophrenic supposed to look like?" To put that question in perspective, we may ask the following questions: What does an obsessive-compulsive look like? What does a bipolar look like? What does a diabetic look like? What does a hemophiliac look like? We could also ask, what does a teacher look like? What does an author look like? What does an accountant look like? After all, a teacher, an author, or an accountant may or may not have schizophrenia!

To determine what a schizophrenic looks like we must say, it depends on the individual and it depends on the current circumstance in which we find that individual. A schizophrenic on medication may look very different from another schizophrenic not taking medication.

Certainly, a diabetic very low on insulin may look like a very different person when he or she has an adequate amount of insulin circulating through the bloodstream. Likewise, a well-rested healthy person may look like a different person when sleep-deprived! When describing a so-called "normal" person, don't we sometimes hear someone say, "He isn't himself today," or "She isn't herself today?"

Remember, one out of every one hundred people you meet has schizophrenia. Have you been able to identify which ones have schizophrenia? Have you been able to pick them out of a crowd at the mall, at the supermarket, or at a sporting event? An honest person must answer "No," to these questions. The answer to the question, what is a schizophrenic supposed to look like, can only be based on preconceived notions, many of which will be incorrect when applied to a specific individual at a particular point in time! Most importantly, it should be noted that outer appearance may often have nothing to do with an internal, biochemically-based illness that you cannot see. So, please don't look at a person stabilized on meds and say, "You do not look schizophrenic on the outside." People with schizophrenia look as normal as anyone else!

Special Notes From The Author

I want the reader to know that the names of some people discussed in this book have been changed to protect their privacy. Also, the names of some people have simply been omitted.

Please note that none of the information presented in this book is to be considered medical advice. Before making any changes to your medical treatment plan, your diet, or your intake of nutritional supplements, always consult with your physician or other health care professional.

I would also like to address the concern that some people have regarding the use of the term "schizophrenic." Although I use the words "schizophrenic" and "schizophrenia" throughout this book, the reader still finds the heading, "Schizophrenia: Let's Call It Something Else!" My mother and I agree that the word "schizophrenia" is scary to us and to many other people as well.

Those who object to the use of the term "schizophrenic" prefer to use words such as "a person with schizophrenia," or "a person who has schizophrenia." I agree that the terms "schizophrenia" and "schizophrenic" should be replaced with words that are less scary and less disturbing; however, both terms are commonly used today, so I wrote this book using words that most people would easily understand.

In addition, we must all recognize that there is a highly successful support group called Alcoholics Anonymous that is widely accepted by people who are grappling with alcoholism. Similarly, there is a support group called Schizophrenics Anonymous that is readily accepted by people who are struggling with schizophrenia, which can be located at the website *www.SARDAA.org*.

Lastly, as indicated on page 10 of this book, I was admitted to the psychiatric ward of a hospital under an Emergency Certificate. Laws vary across the 50 states, but generally an individual can be forced by state law to enter or remain in a mental health facility against his will when an Emergency Certificate is signed by an authorized person. The authorized person is usually an attending psychiatrist, but other mental health workers may also be authorized in some states.

The initial detention is usually for a period of 72 hours. During this time the staff is authorized to observe the individual, conduct an assessment to arrive at a diagnosis, and prepare and implement a treatment plan. If the individual is determined to be a danger to himself, or a danger to others, or is considered to be gravely disabled, the involuntary detention can be extended.

For example, in Ohio a person can be detained involuntarily for 72 hours for observation, diagnosis, and treatment. If deemed necessary, emergency hospitalization may be extended for an additional 48 hours under a TOD or Temporary Order of Detention. During this time period a court will determine if further hospitalization is needed.

For information regarding involuntary detention in a mental health facility in your state, the reader is encouraged to conduct an Internet search. State governments and educational centers have made detailed information readily available to the general public.

About The Author

This work represents Lori Rochat's third edition of her first book titled, *What is a Schizophrenic Supposed to Look Like?* Lori has struggled with the many disruptive problems people face when experiencing the symptoms of schizophrenia. Having overcome many challenges in her life, she now invests her time, energy, knowledge, and experience performing volunteer work on a psychiatric ward, where she shares her insight into schizophrenia with the patients.

Lori earned a NAMI (National Alliance on Mental Illness) Peer-to-Peer Education Program Certificate of Achievement to better serve others who have received the diagnosis of schizophrenia. In 2009 she attended free nutrition classes offered through the Ohio State University Extension program, and earned a Certificate in Expanded Food and Nutrition Education.

While constantly seeking to expand her knowledge of general health, nutrition, mental health, and other important topics, Lori volunteers for the NAMI Speakers Bureau and has given presentations to nurses in training at the Saint Vincent Charity Hospital and Medical Center in Cleveland, Ohio. She continues to seek new ways to educate the public and provide assistance to others who have received the diagnosis of schizophrenia.